Magic of Marketing:

Everything about Delivering Exceptional Customer Delight to Generating Extraordinary Profits

I0464128

Emily Goldstein

Contents

Introduction - What is marketing?

Marketing means customer satisfaction. Marketing is a means to create profit for an organization. Marketing is all about building brands. Marketing is selling. Which one of these will you choose as the true meaning of marketing? If you read carefully, marketing means all the above. Marketing is an amalgamation of various activities which result in a successful transaction. In simple words, marketing is creating a demand for a product or service.

How to create this demand is the art of marketing. In this process, you may have to consider various aspects of the business you are involved in. Effectively dealing with competition is a huge part of your effort. Companies slash prices or follow predatory pricing policies to increase demand. But there is a downside to it – the profit margin suffers. However, low pricing may increase demand and volumes can effectively counter low-profit margins. As a marketing professional, how do you know how the market will really respond to your pricing policies? Your job may be on the line if the strategy boomerangs.

Obviously, pricing alone cannot form a marketing strategy. Maybe you have to look and find the right market segment. Maybe you have to create a new market segment where none exists now. Marketing is a mind game which you have to mater in the first place and device strategies as you go along. The goal posts keep changing. What works today may not work tomorrow. Products have a life – exactly like us. Products go through a life cycle and eventually die. You cannot revive a dead product. For example, there was a time when video cassette recorders were a rage. It was fashionable to play video tapes. Video libraries sprung up at every corner of the earth. Suddenly, technology took a leap. Digital storage became cheap. Content streaming companies like Netflix are now ruling the roost. Do you think you will be able to sell video recorders today? No chance. Marketing professionals understand the dynamics of the market and predict future trends. What will a customer want one year down the line? Two years down the line. Next decade.

To sell you have to understand the customer's needs and wants. The need may be food, clothing, and shelter. Wants may consist of a Porsche or a house with an Olympic size swimming pool. Marketers have to identify these needs and wants.

A large part of marketing consists of branding and advertising, but they cost a bucket of money. How much can you afford to spend on branding and advertising and still make a profit? Remember that you don't have infinite resources. In fact, marketers are often required to work with tight budgets. Money is a scarce resource and has to be spent prudently. What works and what doesn't is a decision which marketers have to decide and your future depends on it. Writing copy is an art which you have to understand if not master.

To top it all, you have social media to deal with now. A single tweet can make or break your brand. Trump tweeted, "General Motors is sending Mexican made model of Chevy Cruze to U.S. car dealers-tax free across the border." The shares of GM plummeted immediately as a result of this tweet. The marketing honchos at GM must have gone into a tizzy before they came up with a clarification. The brand of GM and its reputation was put at stake by a mere 140 characters. This is the power of social media which we are talking about. The news is not all that bad. Social media has now made equals out of everybody. You can have a great impact on sales with social media initiatives even with a small budget. This would not have been possible a few years back. Only companies with deep pockets could afford the cost of advertising.

American Marketing Association has defined marketing as follows: Marketing is the activity, set of institutions, and processes for creating, communicating, delivering, and exchanging offerings that have value for customers, clients, partners, and society at large.

The long and short of it is that the role of marketing is not confined to any single function. Marketers have to manage not only customers but also their channel partners, suppliers, vendors, agents, advertisers and the society at large.

The role of marketing has changed over the years. Marketing function is widely used in many areas. Celebrity marketing deals with selling individuals like CEO's, Movie stars, Musicians, Lawyers and a whole lot of professionals. Event marketing is big business. Did you know that an event like Olympics can involve billions of dollars in marketing? Today, even cities and places are marketed. Think of anything and there is a scope for marketing. Your imagination is the limit.

Generally, whatever be the activity, marketing has some vital characteristics. Market research has an important role to play in successful marketing. You cannot commit millions of dollars to a marketing initiative without proper research. Customer research is another area which needs attention. People, Price, Promotion, Placement, and Product are all aspects which you can ignore only at your peril.

Marketing is no longer an art but also a science. SWOT analysis has become an essential pillar of marketing. SWOT means Strength, Weakness, Opportunities and Threats. You have to carefully analyze each area thoroughly before launching a marketing scheme.

About this book

By this time you would know that this book is about marketing. But it is much more than that. This book contains the essence of marketing. You will gain information which you will get only by reading many books on marketing. Moreover, most of the books use jargon which is used by professional marketers, making it useless for people aspiring to become one. Here, you will come across jargon, but with a suitable explanation.

This book also covers the latest trends in marketing. Modern marketing has transformed into a powerful mechanism with the advent of digital media. You will find an extensive coverage of social media marketing, email marketing, online marketing like PPC ads and organic search. No marketer can be successful without knowledge of modern tools and methods.

Chapter 1: How to build a brand- Making the right impression

What is a brand?

Did you know that the word 'Brand' as used in marketing parlance comes from 'Branding,' It means marking animals with a hot iron to show ownership. Though no hot iron is used in modern day brands, the process is equivalent to passing the test through fire.

There are many definitions of what really constitutes a brand. Essentially, it spells out the unique features of a product or service which separate the men from the boys. What this means is clear. The same product, with exactly the same features, sold by two different companies can have a totally different impact on the consumer depending on the brand value. For example, you will buy a razor made by Gillette without reading the specifications while the same razor costing much less will be up for scrutiny by you. Why? Gillette is a brand which you associate with quality. This is because Gillette has put in a huge amount of effort to build their brand. The key here is the brand and the value it brings to the table. They have created awareness. They have built a reputation. Their name is reflected by their brand.

What really differentiates a brand from the product? A product is essentially produced to fulfill the needs and wants of a person. It refers to the core quality of a product. If you are looking for soap for bathing, any product which fits the definition of soap should work for you. There are no frills or trimmings. If it meets the basic requirements, you can go home after picking up any soap. The question then is why do people go looking for a specific soap? What additional attributes and qualities come into the picture when you choose between various soaps? Why are there hundreds of soap manufacturers catering to a diverse audience? The keyword here is the diverse audience? When you buy soap, you buy into the benefits, both tangible and intangible. You buy the packaging, you buy the smell, you buy luxury. It's no ordinary soap you are going to buy. You are ready to pay a huge premium because of the brand. This brand sets you apart from the rest. It's the total value which you perceive in the soap. You want a rich experience and this is called the brand.

In other words, the basic need can be satisfied by any soap but the intangible benefit which you derive from a particular soap is called a brand. The benefit may be purely emotional or sentimental.

My mom used this soap and so shall I.

I remember using this soap since my childhood.

You notice that happy childhood memories have been associated with the product. This association has been reinforced by the brand name.

Some companies deliver high-quality products and are leaders of the pack. They invest in their brand and become icons in the market. It requires research and dedication to reach this level. Gillette keeps innovating by using razor-edge technology which sets them apart from the competition. Coca-Cola uses a different strategy to create its brand name. It uses imagery and images to create a surreal experience. When you have a Coke you are having an experience, not simply consuming a soda with lots of gas.

Brand and individual consumer

When a consumer searches for a product, he faces many challenges. The product should serve its purpose and should not become defective or unusable. By identifying and associating a brand with the manufacturers, a consumer automatically apportions responsibility to a known entity. Brands convey solidity and guarantee the performance of a product. People know which brands satisfy their needs and which don't. Consumers buy a product when it fits into their need in terms of quality and price. They may not pay for a highly priced product, not because they cannot afford it, but because they do not perceive value in the product which justifies the cost. Brands provide an easy means to consumers to take purchase decisions.

There are other reasons why consumers buy branded goods and products. Buying is a complex process though we do not perceive it as such. Product quality, price point, image and other factors have to be worked out before buying. Many people have been brushing their teeth with Colgate ever since they grew teeth. Imagine what would happen if you did not have Colgate to make decisions for you. You would have experimented with many gels and pastes wasting time and energy. The brand Colgate comes to your rescue time and again whenever you squeeze the last bit of paste from the tube. Maybe you would even experiment with a new brand because these guys have been bombarding you with their messages on television. But then you would be switching brands nonetheless. In technical terms, brands allow you to minimize search costs in terms of decision making and physical exercise.

Brands can have a profound impact on the consumer. The brand is expected to deliver a consistent experience. A brand explicitly conveys the fact that the product that a consumer is about to buy is the same at all times. There is an unwritten pact between the consumer and brand which guarantees the same experience at the same price point and with the same quality and consistency. Consumers will remain loyal to the brand as long as he is satisfied with the experience of buying and using the product. If Gillette can provide the same smooth shave, the consumer will keep buying Gillette razors. This is the reason why it is difficult for newcomers to enter the market. Usually, as long as a person who used to Gillette gets satisfaction, he won't venture into another product. The reason is simple. The risks involved are too many. Who wants to enter the office of the boss in the morning with nicks and cuts on the face? The extra cost is worth every bit of the avoided nick.

Brands also provide self-worth and recognition to a person. Louis Vuitton shoes can elevate your image much more than the size of the heels. Apparel industry thrives on this psychology. You will find big brands in this industry because the value attached to these brands is much higher than say for a GE dishwasher. More because you can't wear GE dishwasher to the office party, can you?

Benefits can be categorized into three main categories. Search goods are those which can be evaluated by their physical attributes like size, color, weight, material, and design etc. Groceries fall under the category of search goods. However, a product like a bicycle stand cannot be assessed visually. Consumers cannot judge the quality, robustness, and durability just by looking at the product. You have to test the product and reach a conclusion. Credence goods are usually associated with services. You cannot evaluate vehicle insurance till your car falls in a ditch and you have to claim insurance. In such case, a consumer will certainly opt for a branded and known insurance company. The brand, therefore, becomes paramount. Essentially, brands become important when the perceived risk becomes more. There are six types of risks which consumers face. Functional risk comes into play when a product fails to live up to expectations. A more dangerous risk comes in the form of Physical risk in which a product is dangerous to the life and well-being of the consumer. Financial risks happen when a product is perceived as overpriced. Social risks occur when a consumer faces derision or ridicule from society. Psychological risks cause mental issues whereas time risk results in loss of time in search for an alternative in case of failure.

Consumers buy branded goods to avoid the above risks. Consumers don't weigh these risks consciously but these factors work in their mind subconsciously. The comfort and safety of brands are an important reason why consumers buy brands.

Brands and their owners

Now you know the value of a brand to a consumer, but what about the people who create the brand? What about the companies who won the brand? Obviously the value of brands to firms is invaluable, otherwise, they would not spend their valuable time and money in building brands.

Brands are the torch bears for companies. They herald the presence of a quality product. Brands reflect the personalities of their owners. Rolls-Royce is a brand which is permanently associated with luxury. Even if the company ceases to exist in the future, the brand will live forever. This is the power of a brand. The Rolls Royce Company has not reached this envious stage by chance. They have deliberately, carefully and diligently built their name over decades. The company legally holds complete intellectual property rights to the brand.

Brand names can be registered as trademarks giving it a legal status. Manufacturing processes enjoy legal protection through patents. Even packaging can be protected through copyrights. Such protection is desirable because firms invest heavily in brands. The fruits of building a brand may take years if not decades. Brands should not get highjacked when they start bearing fruit. Legal protection is therefore necessary for building brands. Many firms make the mistake of not patenting or copyrighting their products and processes. Such mistakes can prove extremely costly in future.

Firms enjoy brand loyalty which in turn ensures the sale of their product. Brands give a unique flavor and meaning to products which are difficult to replicate. It clearly differentiates between one offering and another. Brands enable consumers to make a purchase decision without spending time on searching for a suitable product. Branded products allow a firm to enjoy a steady stream of buyers. The competition has to try very hard because the entry barriers created by brands can be very difficult to jump. Competitive products have to price their products low which result in reduced profits. Soon the competition becomes uncompetitive unless it has very deep pockets.

Brands can be sold for their intrinsic value. They play an important role in the valuation of a company in case of mergers and acquisitions. The premium paid by acquiring companies can be many times the value of a company. Takeover companies buy brands because creating brands is a difficult task which cannot be accomplished easily. Brands take time and effort and therefore paying for them takes business sense. Goodwill created by a brand is of tremendous importance. Companies can build, scale and push sales by riding on the back of brands.

Branding for industrial Goods and Services

We generally associate brands with consumer products. Most of us are aware of consumer goods like Rolls Royce, Apple iPhone, and Nissan Auto. However, there is a huge list of companies which sell industrial products to other companies. Such companies are realizing the importance of branding in this area of industrial goods as well.

Business-to-business products

Sale of goods between companies is termed as a business-to-business market which is growing by leaps and bounds in this past decade. Goods can take the shape of raw materials like adhesives sold by 3M. Who would have thought that adhesives can have a brand name associated with it, but 3M has clearly demonstrated the value of branding. Caterpillar is another example of a

B2B company which has almost become a household name. Siemens is another company which is known for selling industrial products but has created a highly successful brand name.

The advantages of building brands for a Business-to-business entity cannot be understated. In some instances, business brands have more value than consumer products. Branding creates more opportunities for selling because of factors like dependability and timely delivery. Modern day manufacturing advocates minimum inventory. This means lean manufacturing processes which emphasize just-in-time philosophy. Imagine what would happen if a raw material is not delivered on time? It would lead to irreparable losses due to idling manufacturing facility. Companies would rather pay a little more than the average price to ensure timely delivery. Branded companies stand to gain in such a scenario. It would not be an exaggeration to say that companies put their existence at stake when purchasing from unknown entities. They would rather bet on a known supplier than shut their shop.

The rise of the service sector has been phenomenal in the past decade. Services have in fact outperformed sale of goods in terms of turnover. The service sector has been extremely aggressive in marketing their brand. Branson's Virgin airline is a good example. They have racked up the noise to great decibel levels resulting in high visibility. The problem with services, however, is that there are fewer tangibles which you can associate with the brand. Virgin Airlines harps on its economical services – the bed and breakfast type with no frills. But other than the intangibles like quality of service, there is little to boast about in the service sector.

British Airways has taken a different flight trajectory while building its brand. It leans on luxury and first class travel. Notice that Virgin caters to the lowest denominator – the bottom layer of customers while BA goes for the icing on the cake. Both have their loyal customers. Branding for each of them is vastly different: Virgin as a low-cost carrier and BA as a premium airline.

Brand Equity

One of the questions remains unanswered – how do you value a brand? How do you know that your brand has created value? Maybe you could have sold the same quantity without spending on building a brand. Probably, your brand has created value but not enough to justify the expenses. To answer such questions, the concept of brand equity was introduced in the marketing field. This cause more confusion than providing clarity because equity for different people means different things. Measuring brand equity or brand value has been the most important development in marketing. It has spurred companies to commit resources and spend on research trying to understand the subject.

Despite the differences, there is consensus over the fact that branded goods provide better returns than unbranded products. Brand equity is the additional benefit provided by brands to the sale of goods and services. Marketing activities over a period of time result in the development of brands. These brands in return provide added value to a product spread over its product life cycle. This results in a difference in outcomes. There are many ways by which you can create this value for a brand. This brand value which accrues over time can be exploited by a company to increase sales and profitability.

Brand equity also ensures that your competitors cannot enter the same market unless they expend resources equal to the value of the brand itself. This brand equity is much more than the initial marketing effort made by the owners and distributed over a period of time. Monopolies can result from branding activity where a major portion of the market is cornered by one entity.

Chapter 2: Understanding your customer - How to understand the needs, wants and demands of a customer

The customer is king. The customer pays and the buck stops when she pays. This much is true and known. But what motivates a customer to buy and how can marketers influence him or her is a complex task. Marketing at its meanest means focusing on the customer and nothing else. For a marketer, the customer is the bread and butter. How to know the needs of a customer? How to fulfill these needs? What are needs anyway? Needs need not be real. They can be imaginary: just a feeling. It can be a physical need like food, clothing, and shelter. There are other needs like wanting to belong to the community, need to be loved and praised and serenaded. Needs can change depending on the circumstances. It is necessary for marketers to understand the basis of these needs and accommodate them in their product or service. The closer you get to fulfillment, the better your profitability will be

What about wants? How are they different from needs? Wants are desires over and above the needs. Once the basic needs of a person are gratified, he looks to satisfy his desires. Once the hunger is taken care of, a person wants to taste Oysters and quaff Champagne. There is a market for meeting the needs of people and there is a different market to satisfy the wants. Needs are basic – you can't live without them. Wants are more about taste and culture. Some very successful people want to eat McDonald's burgers. It's neither a need nor a great craving. If this same person was living in the South African jungle, a jug of honey would be his ultimate want or desire. Wants, therefore, are a product of our culture and society. Wants transform into demands when there is money in the pocket of a customer. Surplus wealth leads to demands. You, as a marketer, should understand the nature of demands and step in to satiate those demands.

How do you go about the task of understanding the needs, wants and demands of customers? The process is certainly not as simple as it seems. You have to spend an enormous amount of resources and money to access this invaluable information. Marketers spend time pouring over research data in the hope of uncovering facts which would make them successful. However, discovery depends not only on paper trails but also by reaching out to customers personally. CEO's of successful companies stay close to the customer by meeting them and discussing their issues and problems. Marketing professionals must always have their ear to the ground, looking for clues and signs to develop great marketing campaigns.

The market exists not only for physical products but also for services. If you are bold enough, you can even sell the view of Grand Canyon. Does the view belong to you, in the first place? Absolutely not. How do you market the view in that case? Maybe you have purchased a vantage point which offers a stupendous experience to the viewer. Maybe the Grand Canyon looks marvelous from your bird's nest. There is no limit to providing customer delight. You can sell dreams. In fact, marketers often sell dreams – what do you call intangibles but dreams? The point to be noted is that you are not selling a feature of a product but the experience. Your customer buys into the view of Grand Canyon which is an experience. You are not selling the Grand Canyon. It's the same for all products. Marketers make the cardinal mistake of focusing on the features of a product when what they should actually focus on are the benefits. Features should result in a specific benefit. Take the case of an overcoat. Your product may be fabulous and loaded with features. It may be made of quality rubber imported directly from Myanmar but the customer will remain unimpressed. Now go and tell your customers that the overcoat can withstand the wildest storm and still give total protection against rain and sleet. The customer realizes the importance of your overcoat instantaneously. Imported rubber is a feature while protection from rain is a benefit. Focusing on features is also called marketing myopia. Company managements are so much in awe of their product that they go gaga over its features. They do not realize that the consumer gives two hoots to the magnificent features. The customer wants protection from rain, not rubber imported from Myanmar.

Marketers should be able to combine several features and attributes of a product to create customer delight. This means providing an immersive and totally satisfying experience for customers. Savvy marketing professionals know the value of selling an experience. A light bulb is not just for illumination but an aesthetic object which enhances the value of your home. Your car is no longer a machine on four wheels. It transports you into another world of luxury and extravagance. Why do people pay millions and buy a Lamborghini? They can very well manage to travel in an ordinary Ford. The answer is simple. Buyers of Lamborghini spend on the experience, the thrill, and pleasure of driving a luxurious vehicle. They are transported not physically but metaphorically into a different world. Marketing professionals must focus on providing this experience. Of course, not everyone will get an opportunity to market a Lamborghini. But even an ordinary car can be marketed effectively – as much as a Lamborghini.

What's customer Value?

Consumers are a spoilt lot. They have an array of opportunities, options, and choices. They can choose from the many options as long as their need is satisfied. Notice that a customer has to first buy a product before forming an opinion about it. The consumer takes a purchase decision based on expectations and value proposition. The second part of the evaluation depends on the experience one derives from using the product. If the experience is positive, this customer will once again buy your product. Otherwise, he will move on and try another from your competitor. Buyers can be dissatisfied with a product, not because of the intrinsic value but because the product does not meet the expectations. This difference between actual performance and the expectation is the cause for dissatisfaction. Marketers should be extremely careful when they set expectations. If you set low expectations you may not attract enough buyers. The product will not look attractive. The offering will be dull and unattractive. On the other hand, if you go overboard while setting expectations, the buyer will feel cheated and move away from your offering forever. Customer value and customer satisfaction must be at the forefront of a marketer's mind while launching a marketing campaign.

Who is your target audience?

Generally, the market for a single product is huge and cannot be covered in its entirety, unless you have infinite resources. In practice, resources of a company are finite and you have to decide where to spend considering your budgetary constraints. The best way is to divide your audience into market segments. You can then decide which segment is most appropriate for your product and go for it.

Sometimes you may find the whole market attractive and you wish to garner as many customers as possible. A marketer's hope is to generate sufficient demand which can fuel further expenditure on marketing. However, experienced marketers know that this kind of approach is pitted with holes. The customer base is not homogeneous. This means that people have different tastes and not everyone can be satisfied with a single offering. This approach of targeting the entire customer base is therefore bound to fail due to dissatisfaction experienced by one customer group or the other. Selecting a smaller customer base is therefore the way to go.

What is Value Proposition?

Even after securing a great segment for your product, there are other immediate challenges which you may face. The segment you choose may already be crowded and competitors may breathe down your neck. You may escape competition (for a while at least) if you are into niche products. However, niche products may mean a very narrow and small segment where you will find fewer and more demanding customers. There are problems galore wherever you look. You must refine your marketing strategy and find ways to differentiate and position yourself in the market. Differentiation does not mean creating superficial and cosmetic changes. It has to be deep and clear. The customer must feel the difference and be motivated to buy your product even if there are competing products available to him.

Another aspect of segmentation is about cornering the market. This is better said than done. Even within a segment, you will find that your share of the market may be limited. Your marketing campaign should not fall prey to greed hoping to capture the entire segment. If you are lucky, your segment may be large enough to accommodate a big customer base. Your value proposition must be strong enough to set you apart from the competition. Your customer will come to you if you provide this edge in terms of value.

Marketing Conundrums

Marketing is not about products alone. In addition to services, you may be associated with nonprofit organizations, government sector, sports, film, cultural or art management. Every field has some specific objectives and approach to marketing. Profit alone is not a motive in many occupations. Marketing, therefore, assumes a bigger mindshare when you consider the conflicts which may arise while you operationalize your marketing plan. There are five main philosophies which guide marketers. Let us examine each one in detail

Production

The guiding principle of production philosophy is that consumers will queue up to buy your product if it is easily available and at a reasonable cost. This means you must have an efficient production which lowers the cost and a distribution system which makes your product available at every corner store. The customer should be able to grab your product off the shelf without waiting in a queue. Affordability and availability are the keywords here. The production philosophy is simple and therefore popular with marketers. However, there are limitations. Not every product is amenable to easy distribution at low cost. By focusing exclusively on the features of a product, marketing managers lose sight of the benefits to the customer. Customer retention is another problem faced by this approach. In the absence of customer relationship, there is every possibility that people opt for other brands which are competitive. This concept also compels companies to keep their costs low which affects their profit margins.

Product-centric approach to marketing

Consumers buy products and services and are rarely interested in how it is produced. The consumer will opt for products which offer high quality. Here, constant product innovation becomes paramount. You have to keep improving the product by adding new features and improving quality. It is obvious that this marketing strategy is full of pitfalls. Marketers forget their way to success by assuming that the product is king whereas, in reality, the customer is king. This customer wants value, satisfaction, benefits and other intangibles. You may develop a great mosquito killer spray but the customer wants to get rid of flies, it makes a huge difference between success and failure. You may create the best mosquito killer with great features and artistic packaging but you know what would happen when the customer is looking for a benefit which your product does not provide.

Selling Approach

This is the most basic and traditional approach to marketing. Management who do not want to spend money or resources will go for this marketing philosophy. The philosophy is quite simple – promote your product like crazy. Make a big splash. Customers will only notice if you do it in style. You should forget the nuances of marketing. There is no need for subtlety. Just go out and set the market ablaze. Research shows that this philosophy will work only if the product has no clear value proposition and the customer will not think twice before buying.

Selling approach may create sales but it fails to create loyal customers. It goes against the marketing grain because it does not build relationships with the customer – relationship which brings ling term dividend. The focus is on selling the product which is made by the company rather than fulfilling the needs of the customer.

Marketing approach

This is the approach we have been harping on right from the beginning. The focus is on customer satisfaction. The concept fully explores customer needs, wants and demands. Here, the marketer depends on cajoling the customer, coaxing the customer and persuading him to buy the product. There is a pull effect in force. Products are not thrust upon the customer. When a customer willingly buys a product he tends to be loyal. This creates a long-term relationship between the seller and buyer. This yields rich dividend.

Selling vs marketing

Selling and marketing concepts stand at opposite sides of the marketing philosophies. When you are looking at the market from the selling perspective, you perceive the world from the inside. What is your product? What is the production? How to sell to the public? These are the questions you will ask when you are selling. The customer has little role to play in this concept. You manufacture or produce a product and sell it through heavy promotion.

The marketing concept first looks at the customer. It evaluates the demand. It understands customer needs and wants. It then goes on to develop a product which will meet these demands. This enables the company to bond with the buyer. Long term relationships result in long-term profits through repeat buying.

Socially responsible marketing

Marketing philosophies are always in conflict. By fulfilling short-term needs of a customer you may inadvertently damage his long-term interests. Are marketers concerned about the welfare of the community and society as a whole? Do marketers cater to the needs of customers by ignoring long-term benefits or damage? Socially responsible marketing not only focus on the immediate sale and profits but also keeps the welfare of society in mind while developing marketing campaigns. This is also called sustainable marketing. Chemical companies around the world have focused on selling their products by totally ignoring the deleterious effect of chemical on the environment. Many such companies have been stopped from manufacturing poisonous chemical by putting strong government legislations in place.

Customer relationship management

Marketing boils down to customer relationship. This means you derive the full benefit of marketing by delivering unsurpassed customer value, time and again without fail. Customers in any profitable segment are a demanding lot. If you are into selling iron nails and polyethylene bags you can forget marketing and focus on selling. However, in most marketing segments the competition is fierce. Your competitor is equally, if not more aware of marketing strategies. The secret to success lies in implementation. If you are successful in creating satisfied customers you will ensure that these customers come back for more. Making a sale is difficult but retaining customers is tough. Customers will always go for a product which maximizes satisfaction. Value is a result of product quality and cost. Customers compare quality and cost of your product with your competitors and buy from those with perceived higher value. The key word is perception or how a customer views your offering.

Customer-perceived value

In psychology, you will find two words which are relevant to marketing – real and illusion. Real means actual or what exists. However, humans have a great capacity to deceive themselves. We see things which do not exist and ignore experiences which are real. Our perception is more important than reality. Savvy marketers know this truth and work to provide perceived value to customers. Some customers perceive value in a product which provides satisfaction at an affordable price. The actual price does not matter because the cost is compared to the perceived value. A shoe from the corner store will have less perceived value than the one sold by a designer shop. Customers will readily part with their money to buy an exorbitantly costly pair of shoes because of the perceived value. It doesn't matter if the shoes from both the places were sourced from the same place. A designer shop would have paid for this exclusivity and value by spending on advertisements and promotion.

Customer Satisfaction

Satisfaction means you have exceeded the buyer's expectations. A consumer will come out of a shop laughing if she perceives that she got a bargain. That's why discounts and end-of-season sales are so successful. If you notice carefully, the customer is comparing the perceived value of the product with his expectations. If the perceived value falls short of expectations, the customer will be unhappy and dissatisfied. If perceived value matches expectations, the customer is satisfied. If perceived value exceeds expectations, the customer is delighted. The goal of every marketer is to delight the customers.

Studies have shown that a company makes more profit from repeat customers. Brand loyalty is sought after commodity. Marketing professionals know what to do to always keep their big buyers satisfied. Customer satisfaction, brand loyalty, repeat sales, and profitability are intrinsically tied. Your slogan must be to delight customers by exceeding their expectation. There is the fallout of having loyal customers. They bring new customers by spreading the good word. Humans value personal recommendations more than advertisements. You don't have to pay to woo new customers.

Growing Share of Customers

A loyal customer is likely to buy other products sold by your company. Not only do you benefit by capturing customer lifetime value, you also make the customer give you a better share of his wallet. Therefore, there are multiple benefits from loyal customers. Imagine that you are in the business of running a restaurant. You have a choice, either you provide average cuisine at above average cost or delight your customers with the exceptional menu at a reasonable cost. Assuming that you choose the former category. A customer will drop in and since he or she is already there, he or she will order for food. Since there is nothing to rave about, he or she will not visit again. Now let's assume that you go for the second option. The profitability is less but the customer is delighted. The next time around he comes with his entire family. The family recommends your restaurant to friends and relatives who also become your customers. You will keep reaping the rewards for years to come. This is a common secret among restaurateurs – at least the successful ones.

Building the Right Relationships with the Right Customers

No two customers are the same. This is a fact of life. Though you would like to treat all your customers equally, there are compelling reasons why this is not the recommended strategy. Companies should manage customer equity carefully. Customers must be treated as assets which must be optimally utilized. Loyalty is not the only criteria for treating your customers differently. Many loyal customers are unprofitable while some disloyal customers can turn out to be profitable. Have you noticed how different clients are treated differently in a bank? You may fret and fume about the partiality shown by bankers but the fact remains that clients with fat wallets are treated differently. It's not that the bank staff wants to be mean to other clients, it is just that they have been told to spend less time with less profitable ones. A client may be regular but may not have enough profitable transactions. In such a case the expenses on maintaining their account would exceed the profitability. Remember that a transaction cost is attached to every operation. A bank would like to retain and develop a relationship with a client whose transactions lead to profit investments to delight these customers and nurture, retain, and grow them.

Coming back to the marketing scenario it is important to distinguish between a profitable and non-profitable customer. Which customers should you delight and retain? You should classify customers according to their potential profitability and manage relationships with them accordingly. Obviously, you cannot evaluate customers individually. Dividing customers into groups can enable you to manage relationships more efficiently. You should spend more time and effort to provide great service to customers who are loyal and profitable. Customers with mere loyalty without profitability should be given a different treatment.

Conclusion

Understanding the customer is the inflexion point in marketing which demarcates success from failure. Customers are no longer loyal as they once used to be. Online marketing has spoilt them beyond redemption. Customers are showered with heavy discounts and pampered like kids. As a result, customers flit from one brand to another without giving it a second thought. Do you throw up your hand and walk away from it all? In fact, you should pay much more attention to marketing and customer behavior. In this chaotic market, there are many opportunities waiting to be explored and profited from. If you can read even a small portion of your customer's mind you can be a thumping success. After all, humans are also men and women.

Chapter 3: The secret mantra of marketing - The 4 P's + 1

Marketing is the precise understanding of customers and delighting them by delivering optimum products. There are four key elements to marketing _ Product, Pricing, Promotion, and Placement. Each of these elements has to be understood while marketing.

Product

The product is the life of business. Everything, including marketing, must work towards making the product successful. The product can be physical or an intangible service which provides customer delight. Marketers should be able to combine several features and attributes of a product to create customer delight. Long term success of a product will decide the future of a company. It is possible that extensive advertisements can cause a spike in sales of a product. Eventually, customers who consume the product will decide its fate. The product by itself should have the necessary qualities to sustain the market forces.

While developing a product you should first look at the benefits which will accrue to the consumer. Sometimes marketers wrongly focus on the features and overlook the benefits. A customer is not interested in the atomic structure of iron if he is looking to buy a steel walking stick. He would rather look for a product which is light and yet sturdy. The manufacturing process may be unique and use the latest technology to make the walking stick light as a feather, but do not expect the customer to applaud your effort. Give him the walking stick and let him decide its benefits. Rather than focusing on features of the product, it will be better to address the needs of a consumer. When you examine the product from the point of view of needs, you will soon discover the missing parts. Can you provide a good grip? Such questions will come up only if you look from the customer's viewpoint. People using a walking stick would certainly not be healthy and fit. Probably they would like an adjustable walking stick, to cater to individual height. There are many features which you can add once you empathize with the consumer. Your product will be used by humans with feelings and emotions. It will also serve some useful function, but will it delight the customer?

Sometimes marketers want to add frills and trimmings to a product giving it a nice finish, but end up inconveniencing the consumer. A mother of pearl handle would look nice on a walking stick but will it increase the price to an unaffordable level? Will it cause inconvenience to the user? Market research will reveal the answers to these questions. Marketers should understand the eventual use which the product will be put to. The whens and wheres about the product should be analyzed in detail before designing the product.

The manufacturing and production processes are crucial parts of product development. Can the marketing team provide benefits which will impact on the sales? Can you reduce cost by shaving off unnecessary trimmings? Size, color, design, and shape – every small bit matters. You should not overlook a single aspect about a product which can add incremental value. Marketing professionals may be responsible for delivering customer delight by integrating various aspects of a product. Modern packaging materials have revolutionized the industry. Products which are attractively packaged are known to sell more than other similar products rolled in a white paper. You should not overlook nor underestimate the little flourishes which add infinite value to a product. Remember that you are selling an experience.

Product life cycle stages

An understanding of the product life cycle stages is essential to creating durable and effective marketing campaigns.

The product life cycle consists of four stages, each of which has a significant role to play in marketing. The first stage is the Introduction stage. Large FMCG companies like Procter & Gamble have a huge portfolio of products in their stable at different product life cycle stages. New products are introduced to either replace old products or add to the portfolio. The introductory stage is the most difficult period for a product and therefore for the marketing team. Consumers are generally averse to trying new products. This aversion is the very reason why they remain loyal to a brand or product. If you stop selling mature and tested product from the market, the consumer suffers from withdrawal symptoms. Now if you introduce a new product to these customers there may be an initial hesitation in accepting it. It is the duty of marketing department to navigate the product through rough waters. Companies have to spend an enormous amount of resources in launching a new product even though sales are low and the response is tepid. Remember that the owners have already spent heavily on product design and development.

The second stage is the growth stage. This is the time when sales are brisk and the consumer has acted the product. The profit margins which were earlier depressed due to low volumes also picks up on heightened sales. These are happy days for companies and marketers. The initial effort starts paying off and cost of marketing also goes down. The product cruises along smoothly without major effort.

The third stage is the Growth stage in which sales take off and net profits show smart pickup. The production cost is considerably reduced which improves the margins. Marketing activity picks up to spur growth in sales. Product owners can also allocate more money and resources to marketing. With an upswing in profitability, the marketing department gets more funds to ramp up sales. You can call this the prime time for a product.

Consumers at growth stage are used to the product and enjoy the benefits. They need not spend time and energy looking for alternatives. They become repeat buyers. Capital goods also go through the similar life cycle. Products in growth stage show robust sales enabling the company to plough money into the development of new products. You will notice that there is no lull in the development of new products.

The fourth stage is the maturity stage. Products at this stage are cruising along nicely. The marketing effort in the maturity stage is reduced considerably. The product is allowed to sell on its own merit. Sales are however high and companies continue to benefit from these products. Since promotion effort is reduced, the overall cost of product shrinks and profit margins increase.

The last is the decline Stage. In the end, everything has to die and like everything else a product has a shelf life. Products in the decline stage are ready to be retired and replaced by new entrants. The product may become obsolescent or competition may start biting into the sales. Prudent companies do not allow products to die a natural death but give them a decent burial. New products take up space once occupied by products in decline stage.

Price

Price is the most important aspect of marketing. But stop! You read till now that customer is king and customer satisfaction is the ultimate goal of marketing. Do you see a contradiction? There is none. Buyers pay for a product and price is an important factor in deciding whether the buyer is satisfied or not. A great product may fail the satisfaction test if the price is too high. The same product will fail again if it is priced too low. Who knows, maybe the product is not good enough, the buyer may think. To provide buyer satisfaction a product has to be priced correctly. How do you price a product? If the market is flooded with similar products selling at dirt cheap price, you dare not price your product high. Your value will be perceived as low because of the high price. In a way, your competitors decide how you price your product. It is not always possible to undercut or match the price of your competitors. You have to account for various costs associated with the development of a product. You can't go below the production cost or you will incur a loss on every sale. The starting point for pricing a product is the production cost of the product. However, marketing professionals do not come into the picture till the initial problems of production costs and margins are sorted out.

Provided you have the leeway, you would like to price your product optimally – neither too high nor too low. While pricing you must keep in mind that customer does not know the actual value of the product. The pricing should be set depending on perceived value of your product. Alternately, if the perceived value is more than the price, your product will see brisk sales. If the perceived value is lower than the price, you can rest assured that your product will remain on the shelves.

Many factors affect pricing decisions. If your product is riding on a big brand, you can put any amount in the price tag and get away with murder. The perceived value of a product gets a boost when it belongs to a known brand. The brand value gets added to the value of a product and the customer perceives a much higher value. This is the reason why you must nurture a brand.

Some products are price sensitive. A small perturbation in price and the customer behavior becomes unpredictable. You can up the price of such products cautiously. The price to the end customer also depends on the trade channel. Distributors, retailers and channel partners can drum up the price without adding any value. The competition will keep barking and snapping at your heels. You must keep a careful watch on competition and respond to any price change they may introduce in their product. Product discounts can effectively bring down prices and cause disruption in sales in the short run.

Promotion

Marketing without promotion is like winking in the dark. No one knows or cares that you have winked. There are many ways to promote a product. The communication channels vary and depend on the kind of product which you are marketing. A consumer product can be promoted by advertisements on television, magazines, and newspapers. Such products can also be sold directly online through e-commerce websites. Sites like Amazon can sell your products while providing promotion as well. Promotion activities may also include fairs and special discount offers.

Industrial products have to be promoted through different channels. Participation in trade fairs and events related to your product give good exposure. Promotional activity is only a part of the marketing function. Public relations form an important part of your communication portfolio. You have to participate in various activities related to promotion of your product and of your brand.

Placement

There are three things important for a business - location, location and location. The future of your product will be decided by where you place it. Customers should find it convenient to buy your product and should find it in a place where they usually look for it. A customer looking for an evening gown will expect to find it in a boutique if your product is exclusive. The same customer will find similar evening gown in a supermarket. The difference will be in quality and price. Now you have to decide whether to place your product in a supermarket or a boutique. Each will attract different customers. Their choice will depend on the price of your product and quality.

Given that you have a limited stock, the distribution of products plays a critical role. You must have access to the right distributors who will be able to place your products in the right retail stores.

The online channel has lately attracted many businesses. There are many advantages when you sell online. Promotion of products through organic and paid search is much cheaper when compared to traditional channels. You also get access to a huge customer base online. Marketers should look at online channels and use it prudently to increase sales.

These four P's cover all aspects of marketing. However, a fifth P, packaging, has been added tentatively. Smart packaging has become an integral part of marketing and promotion activities. Attractive packaging adds value to a product and improves sales. Some customers buy a product for its packaging.

Chapter4: Market Research – Doing your homework

Before you start a business or launch a product into the market, it is always advisable to do your homework. You must consult the customers as to what they want and whether your product will be received by them well. These issues gave birth to market research fifty years ago and until today has helped businesses to tweak and fine tune their products before launching them into the market. In the initial days, a questionnaire was prepared and market research personnel went from house to house to interview customers about their likes and dislikes. Once all the data was received, the experts tabulated them and prepared a report as to how many people are for the product and what are the inputs they've received from the data. This report gave insight into the minds of the customers and about their needs. This is especially advantageous for foods and beverages and consumer goods like soaps, shampoos and also to service industries.

Today though market research is still the same, thanks to internet online surveys have become more popular than traditional ones. Even car manufacturers and insurance companies are doing market research to learn about customer behavior. Market research enables you to identify new product trends as well as competitive analysis of existing markets. The reports consist of charts, tables, graphs and full reports of customer opinions and choices. Interestingly nowadays even political parties employ market research companies to assess their chances of victory at forthcoming elections.

There are two types of information available for market research; Primary and secondary information.

Primary information can be directly obtained by you from your prospective customers by sending mailers with self-addressed return covers. The customers may fill in the questionnaire and post it back to you. In this age of the internet you can buy email addresses and send emails to customers. Better still, put up the questionnaire on your website and ask them to visit your page and fill the questionnaire. This will enable you to understand how many people are interested in your product and what their response is.

Another form of personal information can be obtained through group discussion and interviews. You may invite a few of the customers for a group discussion about your product. Give them sample products to use. Only then people will be interested in attending.

As for the secondary information, you can buy mobile numbers from phone companies and send text messages. Several malls and commercial places ask their customers for phone numbers. You can take those data's. Educational institutions like universities conduct several surveys. They have a wealth of information. You can collect that data also for your market research.

Address the issues that are voiced by your customers to make the product robust. Take the case of Dove beauty soap. Their target audience is women and if you see their advertisements they use real people to market their product. No model or actress is used to endorse Dove. Why? It's not that the company cannot afford to pay for an actress. The reason is this;

The company conducted a market survey where many women had said that actresses modeling for soaps made them feel insecure. Moreover, the women felt that the soap must be expensive. Also, they felt that this soap is for rich and famous and not for common people. When these facts were kept in front of the company professionals they changed their advertising strategy and started using real people. They made a request through newspapers to all the women to send their pictures so that they can be featured on Dove advertisement. Believe it or not their sales plummeted and increased tenfold after they used real people to model for their commercials. This is how useful market research is to assess, analyze and arrive at the right target audience and tweak your campaign to suit customer needs.

By using brainstorming tools for getting information on product ideas, buying preferences, and purchasing decisions among certain population companies are able to arrive at the right answers to sell their products.

Why is market research important for business?

1.   To understand customer needs

2.   Identify problem areas and fix it

3.   To develop effective strategies

Once you've done your homework, priced your product competitively, and advertised it, you can hear the jingle of money. But is this enough? Well no.

You have to keep at it as times are fast changing. Every few years your product will need an up gradation as customer's interests will shift as new competitors enter the market. It is here that once again you'll have to conduct market research to know your strengths and weakness and how you can overcome it.

Even new regulations and government legislations will have to be taken into consideration. It is here that you need to make wise decisions. Otherwise, your company will be finished. Understanding emerging trends is very important for the success of a product.

If you're a startup then market research is all the more necessary. Here is the case of Café Coffee Day, a local brand in India who couldn't match up to Starbucks. Though Starbucks coffee is more expensive than Café Coffee Day cappuccino, still customers were thronging Starbucks and not the other coffee shop. Intrigued, they conducted a market survey to find out where the problem was. To their surprise, customers said that the ambiance in Starbucks is way better and also the cup's shape is more attractive. Immediately Café coffee day redid their interiors and changed their cups and also started offering snacks just like Starbucks does. Viola! The crowd started to walk in and today there are more café coffee day outlets than Starbucks in India. Each person who answered their questionnaire got a 50% off coupon at one of their outlets and these free coupons helped them to get more insights from customers and also foot falls.

This is the power of market research. It can help you to identify your lacunas and correct them instantly. The secret here is being innovative and generous. You're likely to be rewarded.

Chapter 5: What is digital media marketing?

SEO (Search engine optimization)

These 3 words have created a storm in the 21st century. They've changed the course of how marketing is done in the traditional way till now. Search engine optimization has helped thousands of businesses get noticed online to market as well as sell their products online. The infamous JC Penny episode that happened a couple of years ago during festival time is proof for this. By manipulating SEO strategies JC Penny appeared on the front page of Google search for all products searched online. They made a whopping $35 million only during the festival time of December. This is proof that internet marketing is the mainstream marketing for the present and future.

SEO is an ongoing process of making a website and writing content that is related to people who are looking for information regarding a product or service. Search engines send a web crawler to search for content and display it on the search results page. Search Engine Optimization (SEO) is the process of improving the volume or quality of website traffic from 'natural' or 'organic' searches by tweaking various elements of the website to optimize it.

SEO includes two distinct and important aspects which need to be addressed if the optimization is to be successful. The first is the technical aspect (such as keyword research, site architecture, use of keywords in titles and meta tags, site navigation for web spiders, incorporation of site map and directory, building links etc). These technical features make it easier for search engines to find and index a site for the appropriate keywords. The second aspect relates to marketing-focused tasks to make a site more appealing to users (content, layout, images, easy navigation for visitors, function tabs or buttons e.g. 'add-to-favorites', 'refer-a-friend', 'quick inquiry' etc, that are easy to access and operate and so on).

SEO strategies can be learned but need a lot of hard work, dedication and a will to experiment. However, SEO is a complex issue but it is worthwhile and budget permitting to hire an expert SEO consultant to market your website.

Google Analytics

Google has analytics that can help you gain knowledge on what the highly searched keywords are on Google. For example, say you have a website and you are selling shoes, then your keywords will be running, jogging, walking, shoes and so on. You will also have secondary keywords like comfort, footwear, feet, etc. You need to add meta tags and attractive keyword infused titles for each shoe. The description of the shoe should also consist of keywords. All this will help to optimize your web page. Say someone is searching for shoes online, then your website will appear. You may argue that there are hundreds of sites selling the same product. How will your site appear? Well, that is where you need to keep updating your site with the latest information as well as use geographical location specific copy.

Keywords may be of various types. One classification may be single-word, multiple-word, and theme-based keywords. Another may be in terms of the type of search they predominantly support depending on how potential customers key in their search terms i.e. broad-match, phrase-match, exact-match, or negative match. Still, another may be a target market specific classification such as 'business-specific', 'service-specific', 'geographic' or 'general' keywords.

Geographic keywords

Geographic targeting (with the use of geographic keywords) can be very useful for organic search results as well as for pay-per-click (PPC) advertising if the product-market matrix requires such targeting. For instance, in the case of organic searches, it is sometimes possible to get first-page results on Google by including the name of the city or state to the page title and content. In the case of PPC, geographic keywords help in taking advantage of 'long tail' keywords to drill down into very specific geographic queries.

Business specific keywords

Business websites should not only be user-friendly, they must also be search engine friendly. An effective strategy to achieve this when using business-specific keywords is to incorporate business specific keywords as search engine friendly naming conventions for web pages. Business specific keywords are mostly long-tailed keyword phrases. They may likely reduce general traffic to a business website for organic searches or the display frequency of pay-per-click (PPC) ads, but users entering specific keywords are typically more likely to buy; being in the final stages of the buying decision. Business-specific keywords will also help increase the search engine rankings of a business website.

General Keywords

General keywords help to get a lot of 'hits' to your website. The crowd that visits your site is potential buyers but is not ready to buy immediately. They are the kind who is browsing the net for initial looking up of all products related to their specification. Only when they search for specific keywords will you know that there is going to be a sale. General keyword search is good for search ranking of your website as well as good ROI (return on investment).

Meta Tags

Meta tags are small lines that are written in HTML code placed between headers. For example < header >. This describes the website to the search engines. Meta tags let the search engine know about the web page and help the spider to crawl effectively throughout the page. If properly used, meta tags can help the ranking of a site as well as drive traffic.

Link Building

Link building is another important aspect of SEO. You don't get all the traffic from organic searches. People visit from other sites as well. If your site can have external links from other sites that'll help in improving SEO and also smooth navigation. Internal links from one page to another on your website will improve traffic to all pages. This can usually be best achieved by embedding the links in specific keywords or phrases i.e. including the right keywords in the anchor texts of the links. This also increases quality traffic and improves conversions.

Low-quality links can affect your ranking and SEO. The external links should be from reputed sites so that your ranking also improves. The links you get should be relevant to your site. It shouldn't be that you're selling shoes and your external links are from a doctor's website. Relevance is the keyword here.

Google keeps changing its parameters from time to time for SEO. What was relevant two years ago is no longer of use. There was a time when article directories were in vogue. Getting back links from Ezine articles and other such sites became a norm till Google de-recognized all the directories. Overnight hundreds of websites lost their ranking. From PR 5 they fell down to PR1. Then came guest posts. Blogs started accepting guest posts and giving back links in return. Google realized that blogs were taking money and posting posts that have the least relevance or no unique information that was also chucked.

Presently AdSense makes sense. Pay Google and get noticed. This monopoly needs to be curtailed. That is why Yahoo and Bing are also offering search. But they aren't as popular as Google. Facebook is also trying to enter the search market.

Every six months there is something new in the anvil. This is what makes it exciting.

Use of PPC & its place in marketing

Online shopping has seen a steady increase in popularity as almost the entire world is familiar with the internet. The global economic meltdown that occurred a few years ago gave an added fillip to this trend as consumers adapted to online shopping to cut down expenses; often at the cost of high street stores. This shift in consumer preferences has, in fact, led to a marketing revolution of sorts, as more and more businesses (at least the ones that are search engine savvy) increasingly switch marketing and advertising budgets from the old-fashioned magazine, newspapers, and television to the internet where you need to pay only for Pay-Per-Click services or PPC.

While shopping online, a visitor may (or may not!) click on your Ad which appears on the search engine results page or a web page (also termed a 'Landing page') which he has reached (or 'landed' on) by keying in his search keyword or phrase. Pay-Per-Click (PPC) works on the principle that you (the advertiser) pay a predetermined price (or bid amount) to the search engine provider only when a visitor clicks on your Ad. PPC traffic can be accessed (purchased) from specialized PPC search engine operators. There are, literally, hundreds of such providers available on the net, but it's advisable (and safer) to choose one of the leading (though somewhat costlier) sponsors such as, for instance, Google, Yahoo! or MSN.

The use of PPC has become very popular with both merchants and affiliates (who promote products and services of others i.e. of merchants/ vendors) as a promotional tool in internet marketing. PPC search engine marketing is aimed at driving targeted traffic (potential buyers) to a website promptly and efficiently; and provides speed, flexibility, and economy not only to vendors, affiliates and website sponsors but also to consumers. One of the greatest advantages of PPC is that, unlike other types of advertising and marketing, the Ad is presented directly to the target market. This greatly increases the chances of a better return on investment as compared to other more conventional advertising modes.

Using PPC does not mean that the traditional 'marketing mix' should be overlooked (as many businesses, unfortunately, tend to do). In fact, the 4p's of marketing (product, place, price and promotion) are as important in internet marketing and PPC advertising as any other marketing strategies; particularly in the present economic environment. The product (or service) being offered should be saleable and should be such that promotion through search engine marketing (SEM) is possible. The website should be 'optimized' so that the place at which the Ad is displayed on the search results page is high enough (based on a combination of factors beyond the scope of this discussion) to attract attention but still economical (the click price rises for higher displays). And, of course, the price point should be compatible with the product, place, and promotion (and competition!)

Using PPC also does not mean that you abandon all other traditional marketing strategies. PPC may be a very important instrument in building up your business, but it certainly is not the only one; it should be just one implement in your marketing tool box! While PPC advertising has many advantages (it efficiently directs quality traffic – people who are already searching for your product category to your website), it can very easily become uneconomical (as competition for your keywords increases, with a consequent increase in click rates). Sometimes, your product may be such that while PPC advertising works, more traditional marketing strategies may work better and be more profitable.

Hence, your advertising and marketing strategies should always be a judicious mix of the traditional methods and PPC advertising, where PPC is just one important component of your marketing armory.

Chapter 6: SWOT Analysis

Products become successful or they fail because of many reasons. The product itself may be very good but it may still fail. The product may be mediocre and it may bring windfall gains to a company. You have to understand the forces which come into play when you plan to launch a product in the market. This analysis is called SWOT. Strengths – Weaknesses – Opportunity – Threats. Strength and Weaknesses are internal to an organization. They are therefore simpler to examine and evaluate. Opportunities and threats are external to an organization. They are difficult to access and much more difficult to manage.

Should you fit your product into the SWOT mix or should you evaluate a product by doing a SWOT analysis on it? The question is far more complex than it seems. The decision may depend on many factors. By and large, SWOT is done on an existing product or service. Another perspective is to look at SWOT analysis as an attempt to find the right opportunity for a company given its strengths in a given market environment. There may be many opportunities but the resources may permit you to pursue only limited options. Using SWOT analysis you will be able to arrive at the right product for your company.

Let's look at the various components of SWOT in more details.

Strength

Strength means your positives. Does your company have advantages over the competitors? If so, you begin your venture on a high. The advantage may be your technological skills which you bring to the table. You are able to manufacture a product which is better because of its unique features. Maybe you have access to resources which are scarce. You know here to buy the raw material which is cheaper and of better quality. Do you see how this can give a competitive edge? All these factors can be summed up in one word – your USP. What is your unique selling proposition? Do you have a USP in the first place? If so, this becomes your strength. You can confidently go ahead and invest your money and resources because you know your strength.

Strength can also mean competitive advantage. You can have resources in form of capital, existing customer base, excellent relations with suppliers who can extend credit line or you may have patents which can be invaluable assets. All these are your strength. Sometimes people are your biggest strength. You may have a great team with unique abilities and qualifications. It is easy to overlook people as your strength. However, on many occasions, a mediocre product can become a winner when handled by the right marketing team. You may have great production setup which can churn out products that are cheaper and better than what the competition can provide.

You may have noticed that the strengths have an intrinsic value. They would still be intact even if you are hit by a hurricane. Your factory may go under water, your raw material may become soggy and unusable but the customer base will remain intact. Your line of credit will not be affected by the hurricane. You may sustain a temporary loss. You may even close down your factory. Still, your strength would remain.

Strengths, therefore, are internal to your organization. It defines your intrinsic value. Your product or service will be built on your strength. They show the way. They are essential features, without this, your product will not be successful. Every product or services should be based on your strength – whatever it may be. Even a single positive factor can trigger a success. You should, therefore, be able to define your strength properly. Vague and diffused concepts cannot be considered as strength. You can use your competitors as an example. 'I can deliver my Pizza to your home in half an hour '. This looks like your strength. But what if everyone offers delivery of pizza in half an hour? What was your strength is no longer so because it is no longer a unique offer. Now you know how to formulate your strength.

Weaknesses

Weakness does not mean you are dead. It just indicates that you have to be careful and cautious. You should not run away from enumerating your weaknesses. If you have built a product, you look at it like your baby. It's flawless. It's beautiful. You get carried away by its beauty and you overlook its flaws. You spend money and resources to produce more of these babies or products. But your customer is a ruthless guy. He does not like the nose of your baby. You knew it was a flaw but you glossed over it. Your customer will not be as forgiving as you. Had you accepted the fact that your product has flaws, you could have done a great nose job and corrected the issue before launching your product. The questions which you have to answer are whether there are weaknesses. If so, how can you correct them?

Weaknesses arise from within. They are not external forces which you have to face. They can, therefore, be anticipated and corrected. If this is not your first market launch, you can always ask your customers about the new product. Customers usually don't lie because they are not in love with your product like you are. They don't benefit from telling lies. There is no incentive for your customers and therefore you are likely to get a truthful appraisal.

Your competitor is your best friend. Look at his product and compare yours. Can you eliminate any weaknesses which you can observe? Is your product superior to your competitors in all aspects – quality, packaging, look and feel? Can you do better than this? Competition, once again, will not lie. You can easily pick your weaknesses when you put your product directly in front of the competition. You can learn lessons from your competitor without paying a single dollar. Learning your competitor means correcting their flaws when it comes to your product. Simply do one better than your competitor and your weakness will become your strength.

Weakness can come in different forms. Do you have sufficient funds to market your product? If not, you should shore up your finances. You can't rectify this weakness when you are in the middle of the marketing battle. Your supply chain must likewise be tested. A weakness here can lead to your doom. Weaknesses in the organization are the most difficult to identify. Management does not like to face issues and problems. Senior management will die before admitting to any weakness. This is usually the downfall of a company and its product.

You must face weaknesses boldly. You should not ignore problems but tackle them immediately. Timely action can turn your weakness into your strength.

Opportunities

Opportunities are external to an organization. You will find opportunities lurking are in corners and dark places. They are therefore difficult to spot unless you are sharp and vigilant. Good marketers watch trends carefully. Who thought that water, a resource which is freely available, can be sold in bottles? But the company which sold bottled water first made gold out of water. This was an opportunity which everyone overlooked. But sometimes opportunities are linked to a place, an occasion, an event or time. If someone had tried to sell water in bottles (or jugs) a hundred years ago, he would have been laughed out of business. Opportunities are therefore tenuous and linked to time.

Technology is a great place to look for opportunities. Disruptive technologies like the internet have revolutionized life. Netflix took the bull by the horn and started transmitting videos through the internet. Video libraries simply vanished into thin air due to Netflix. E-commerce has changed the way we do business. Amazon started by selling books online. It is one of the biggest retailers in the world today. The best part is that Amazon does not make or store a single product.

Technology is, therefore, the best hunting ground for opportunities. Look at the supply chain management today. Products can be moved around the globe without batting an eyelid. Apple iPhones are manufactured in China and sold in America. Some products are manufactured in several locations, assembled in another country and sold in a different country altogether. Low cost of labor has driven manufacturers to China even though transportation costs have to be borne by them.

Your product will eventually be purchased by a person. Changing social trends can be a huge opportunity. Small cars became a fashion which directly affected the big three in America. Ford, Chrysler, and GM lost the game when they continued selling the dinosaurs. Japanese car companies made the best out of the new fad. It is a different matter that dinosaurs are back in fashion but the car paint on these three companies has long faded away.

Government policies change like the proverbial weather. There are huge opportunities waiting to be exploited in these changes. However, you can't predict these changes and therein lies the problem.

Threats

If only you knew. Threats come from the outside. They are the enemy who strikes without notice. Ironically, technology, which provides great opportunities, is also the biggest threat to companies. You may applaud Netflix for taking over the home movie market, but what about the video libraries. They lost badly and hold technology as the biggest culprit. Technology causes the biggest disruptions in society. If nothing else, you have to look out for technology changes and take appropriate action before you get wiped out. The internet has spelt the doom of many traditional businesses. Take the example of greeting cards. Once upon a time, printing and selling greeting cards was a dream business. Archies was a big name in those days. What happened to Archies?

Government laws and policies can trip a business overnight. Customs duty on components can drive up the overall cost of a product and make it unviable. Prices of raw materials can upset your cost structure. Take the example of crude oil. In mid-2008 oil hit $139 a barrel. It started slipping and tanked to $38 by end 2008. Many companies made a fortune and many folded up, never to be seen again. Such is the power of external forces.

Since threats are external, you have no control over them. Does it mean that you smile and bear with threats? You must be prepared for all eventualities. Marketing professionals have a vivid imagination. They can think of the worst case scenario like no other. Make a list of the worst that can hit you. Make your imagination run wild. Think of doomsday. Once you have a list of the worst, make a contingency plan. How will you deal with the catastrophes? Remember that your competitor will be in the same thick soup as you. You will survive if you can keep your head above water.

Work on your SWOT! Create a winning strategy. You will at least get a glimpse of the future and what it will look like.

Chapter 7: Primal Attraction – How to write a Copy

In the end, the message is you. People remember your company, product or service by your advertisements and this means Copy. Marketing, in essence, boils down to good copywriting skills. Some say that writing copy is an art. Others claim that it is a science. The truth probably lies somewhere in between. One thing remains constant is – rigorous and systematic study of the product or service. What are the steps in writing a mind blowing copy?

The target customer group

Copywriting brings images of crazy guys sitting in remote places and working their magic. In practice, this is a false image. Writing copy is more about identifying the right market segment, researching the target market, understanding the needs of the buyers and finally coming up with a mind blowing message.

There is no point in identifying your target by putting them in an age group of 15-45. This means nothing. Get near your audience. Feel their need. Understand their pain points. This can be done only through personal contact. Sitting a thousand miles away and writing copy for an audience you don't know is going to result in failure. You must get as close to the buyer as is possible. Close does not mean physically close. You don't have to get physically intimate. You have to get into the mind of your target audience by observing their behavior first hand.

Research is the foundation of great copy. You can get to know your audience in finer detail if you do some serious research. Imagine if you want to understand a movie buff. Generally, you will not find this creature roaming the streets because most probably she will be glued to her television or PC screen. When you get closer you will notice the idiosyncrasies of a movie-crazed audience. Speak to a couple and you will know what kind of a world they live in. You will get a zillion ideas when you actually meet up with the real guys and gals out there. They will provide you all the material you need to get into the zone.

Copy need not be and should not be in-your-face. The message always goes through when you address the needs of a person. Sensitivity and thoughtfulness always win. Your copy will be a success in proportion to how your writing resonates with the target audience. Personal care products must carry a subtle but focused message. The idea is to create an impact on the minds of people. Splashy, wild and gaudy messages may look great but they drive away the target instead of attracting them.

What is your message?

Remember that your message always comes first. You will be tempted by an idea which seems out of the world – and it surely is. You don't want an out of the world idea. You want a down to earth message which resonates with your audience.

The message has to be clear and unambiguous. You should not cram messages in the hope that something will strike a chord with the audience – it won't. If your message means several things to several people, it will not work.

You should keep your message focused and to the point. For example, copy for a face cream can address several issues. It may clear the skin. It may remove pimples. It may moisten your dry skin. There are many intended uses for a face cream. There may be a huge audience for each of these solutions. Should your message reach out to the whole group encompassing the entire range of problems? It is tempting to create an all-embracing message but it will only lead to an all embarrassing result. A person with dry skin wants a solution to his problem. This person is not interested in a clear skin. She is not worried about pimples. When this person comes across your message, she is not sure what you are offering. The real message gets lost in the melee. Do you think this person will buy your product, especially when she gets a definite message that another face cream will solve her problem?

You should avoid the trap of an all-encompassing message. Focus on what is the best feature of your product. Keep at it till your message is loud and clear. Do not waver from your message in the middle of your campaign. Avoid all temptations. The problem with copy is that many professionals accept defect right when they are on the verge of victory. Advertisements are costly. Spreading the word is expensive. It is also a long haul business. There are no shortcuts. Sometimes business owners think that a couple of television slots is all it takes to get customers. They allocate a small budget for advertising and when things don't take off they blame the Marketing guys. As a marketing professional, you must make it clear to your client that advertisements cost money and plenty of it. Your marketing budget should be large enough to take a short term beating. Some companies like

McDonald's have taken decades to promote their brand.

What is your brief?

A brief is what your client tells you – not something which you imagine. If a product X is cheap and the brief is to convey this message, don't go on and rave about its great features. The best that can happen is that your client will shoot it down in your very first presentation, provided that your client knows what he wants. Unfortunately, clients themselves are clueless about the logic of copywriting. As a result, you land with a useless message which extols the benefits of a product while the main benefit, in this case, low cost, is lost in the maze. A bad advertisement campaign can lead to irrecoverable losses. You can get up, dust your pants and start afresh. The customer buying your product is already confused and will refuse to accept a new message. It doesn't work.

It is, therefore, essential to listen carefully to your brief. Pick a single, most important feature of the product and then bang it into the audience incessantly. Hoardings, TV commercials, newspapers, magazines, blogs, website, AdWords... .everything should carry the same message. It should scream, MY PRODUCT IS CHEAPER THAN ANYONE ELSE'S IN THE MARKET!.

The big picture

Great copy is not poetry or literature. Effective copy gets you results – sales – profits. You have to put in a great deal of thought while planning your campaign. Advertising companies often face a conflict between the planning department and the creative guys. The role of accounts, planning, and copy is different but they come together to create a message. Everyone in the advertising department must understand the role of other parts which form the whole.

To be effective, a marketing professional must know the big picture. The message must be real and impactful. For this to happen, you must plan carefully, do your due diligence in the form of research. You have to put your copy in context. What is your message? Are you able to capture this message in a few words? Can you cut some more words from the copy? Does your message embody the brief? If you can answer in the positive to all these questions, you have a great copy.

Sometimes, a campaign may not take off in spite of the best copy. This may be due to other reasons. Customers may not actually like the product. The product may not come up to expectations. Your clients do not have a good reputation in the market. There are many reasons why your copy may not work.

Writing copy for the net

The internet has overturned the copywriting applecart in many dramatic ways. If you look at the PPC or Pay Per Click market, the emphasis is on keywords. Your product or service will appear on web pages only if you use the right keywords. This peculiar requirement has led to many ridiculous and absurd messages. Copywriters and marketers must learn to live with keywords by creating unique messages which contain keywords in relevant messages. Google, the main player in PPC space provides guidance on how to create copy for online advertisements. Every marketer must understand Google requirements in order to survive in this modern world.

Writing articles and blog posts for the promotion of goods and services has become a norm. Marketing professionals must know what works on the net and what doesn't. Remember that the market has moved to the virtual world and you must learn to live with it. You are now competing with search engines. These machines look for keywords, catchy headings, optimization and much more. Copy is no longer about words but keywords. In a way, the internet teaches you to write copy which is relevant and to the point.

Copy is marketing in a few words

Ultimately the message is you. Marketing ends in copy. Grabbing the eyeballs is the challenge when you consider that the world has become a crowded space. You are chasing a knowledgeable customer who can't be fooled into buying your stuff. The internet has posed new challenges to marketers. It has also brought big rewards. In this big bad world, there is one thing which has remained constant – COPY IS STILL THE KING OF MARKETING!

Chapter 8: Leveraging social media – Facebook, Instagram, and Twitter can help in your business

Ten years ago when twenty-one-year-old boy Varun and his two other friends were at university, they were famously known as the backbenchers. Laid back and not getting great grades, they felt that they may not be able to get good placement. But there was a fire in them to start a business, make money and become famous. Yet they were clueless as to what their product would be or how they'll market it. Varun's cousin brother visited him for vacation and Varun saw him proudly sporting his alma mater's name on his sweatshirt. Varun thought how wonderful it would be to wear a T- shirt or sweatshirt with your school or college name on it? Weren't school days the most memorable days of our lives? This brilliant idea took him on a trip to a nearby town that was famous for outsourcing clothing to the USA and other western countries. He approached a dealer and asked if he could print sweatshirts and T-shirts for him. The dealer readily agreed and offered to help. Varun wondered how to go about the whole thing. He then met with the principal of his school and requested permission for him to print their logo on T-Shirts and sell them at the school fest. Since Varun was well known in school, as he was their basketball team captain the principal didn't find anything wrong in allowing him to sell at school. After the school's logo was printed on the shirts, The first hundred sweatshirts sold instantly and that gave Varun the zest to go online and start an e-commerce website for printing institutions logos on shirts. That is how www.almamater.store.in came into existence.

Varun was the first to promote his product through Facebook for free. He tagged his friends who tagged theirs in turn and that in turn made him reach out to more than a million people through Facebook. He employed 20 people whose job was just to tag people on Facebook. His product was one of its kind and all the students who were alumni of their respective schools ordered for their sweatshirt. In a year's time, Varun received venture capital funding of two million dollars and was adjudged as the best startup in the country. He received many awards and today his company ships around 20,000 units in a month.

This is a real life story of Indian-born Varun Agarwal who became an entrepreneur at the age of 23, thanks to social media. Facebook, Twitter, Instagram, YouTube are powerful tools that can help you to promote a product for free. Ten years ago they were clueless as to how anybody could make money through social media. It is people like Varun who showed the way. When Mark Zuckerberg, the founder of Facebook came out with a public issue there was no way he could monetize Facebook. But over the years he and other social media entrepreneurs realized the power of this medium and learned to monetize them. Today Mark Zuckerberg is one of the top 10 richest men in the world.

The truth is, social media is here to stay and has transformed the way the world is communicating today. A single tweet can simply bring down a government. Such is the power of social media. Prime Ministers and Presidents of countries are on Twitter reaching out to people on a daily basis. Video sharing platforms, blogs, websites, and e-commerce are helping customers connect with their favorite products. Social media has changed the way marketing is done; from monologue to multilogue. It enables customers to directly deal with companies and vice versa. There are no rules for social media. The direct interaction you have with your customers can build brand loyalty and brings repeat customers.

Even a small scale business can be marketed through social media. Whether you're selling clothing, edible or beauty products, anything and everything can be sold here. Did you know that mobile phones are the largest selling product online? According to Amazon.com, every second they're selling a mobile phone. Such is the power of internet marketing and social media. Since people are able to get Facebook and Twitter on their phones, you as a business is connected 24/7's with your customers. Just get yourself up there and start promoting your product. You're sure to be heard.

Facebook tops in promotions

Facebook has more than a billion users. It is humungous and is a world in itself. Advertisers are salivating to make use of this outreach and Facebook is also taking advantage of it. They've started to auction their advertising space. You can easily promote your products on Facebook for a small fee. They help you to be seen by targeted audience. The keywords help to find the right type of people who'll be interested in buying your product. On the right side of each profile keyword, specific products are displayed. If you click on a product you wish to know about, it takes you to their website. The advertiser only pays per click. It is affordable and easy to advertise through Facebook.

There are many beauty tutorials, cookery and several other products that are marketed on YouTube. Thanks to an online platform, tutoring has taken a different twist altogether. www.khanacademy.com is one of the most popular online tutors for education. Be it SAT or high school math and science subjects you can find help here. Sitting at home you can learn from this website. Khan academy has assets worth 60 million dollars. Microsoft chairman Bill Gates teaches his kids through Khan Academy. That is the power of social media which has taken the world by storm.

Even traditional products like cars are unveiled through social media. Whether it is to sell a product or a musician, everything and everyone is marketed through social media. It is free to promote. Simply take a video and upload. We all know the story of Justin Beiber. A video of his single earned him more than a million views making him a start overnight at the age of 13. Today film promotions are done through Facebook, Twitter, and YouTube. Within an hour you can easily get a million views i.e. if your product is excellent and interests the viewer. You can also share the link on your other social media accounts.

Facebook offers live video. This makes it all the more interesting and interactive.

Tweet your product on Twitter

Twitter is another medium that helps you to connect with the world. President-elect Donald Trump used Twitter to broadcast and campaign before elections. It is very easy to connect with people on Twitter. Find like-minded people and follow them. You'll see that people will also follow you. When you are launching a product, make announcements on Twitter. With one tweet you can reach your target audience. It reaches instantly. Have a BUY NOW tab on your timeline. In just a few tabs, people can buy your product. See to it that you maintain customer relationship. Have reviews and testimonials on your page.

Turn Instagram into your digital store

The difference between other social media's and Instagram is it doesn't allow you to hyperlink. Also, it is more visual than copy. The pictures are square and they've to be breathtaking. Celebrities like Selena Gomez have more than 100 million followers on Instagram. She endorses more than fifty products on her Instagram profile. Kylie Jenner who has more than 80 million followers markets her lip kits and cosmetics through her profile. Sync up your inventory directly to your Instagram account and it'll act like a catalog for you. Shopseen is an easy to use application that can turn your Instagram account into a digital store. Just link the two and once it is confirmed start adding images of your products. From there you can add in descriptions and prices. Payments can be made using credit cards on a secure server and the customer follows through your profile link.

Social media has seen to it that they're very much a part of your business campaign right from the start. They also are able to give inputs in the form of reviews and are involved in developing a brilliant product that will be useful to them. Marketing on social media has advanced making the customer come back and buy more. You can cross promote your Instagram sale through other social media platforms like Facebook, Pinterest, Tumbler, Twitter, etc. Today consumers are not inaccessible anymore.

Chapter 9: Harnessing the power of email – Email marketing

With the advent of the internet, marketing took a new dimension online. Suddenly there was a great rush by small and medium companies to be seen and heard. Every business started a website and thought that they've made themselves heard. But did that get them more business? Sadly no. That is when emails became a tool for marketing.

Email marketing is one such tool which has helped several businesses to kick up sales. Email marketing has evolved within the last 15 years. What started out as a simple newsletter is today transformed into video messages, mobile marketing and SMS and text marketing as well. Ideally, email marketing involves sending messages through emails to prospective customers. They can be in the form of advertisements or newsletters soliciting business for your entity. Through email marketing, you can also build trust and loyalty with your product. It also helps in creating brand awareness.

In the first few years, email marketing wasn't as effective as it is today due to lack of reach. With the arrival of smartphones, every individual has an email id and the reach has spread far and wide. With a single email, you can grow your business into a million dollar company. Seriously, that is the power of email marketing today. There are innumerable advantages to email marketing. They are:

1.   Ease of use

2.   Its Cost is nominal

3.   It Reaches the wider audience

4.   It is interactive

5.   It is data driven

6.   It Targets multiple audiences

•   It is really very easy to use email marketing. You don't need specialized tools to do it. Your personal computer is good enough. You don't need salesmen to go door to door. Technology is easy to use and anybody can use it to send emails. Email marketing eliminates middlemen. There are inexpensive software's that can help you to send thousands of emails in one go and also keep track of how many are opened and who all have seen it. These software's are easy to use; they'll help you to keep track of your email marketing campaign.

• It is inexpensive to use email marketing for your business. The expense is negligible. Print, television, and telephone marketing costs money. You've to pay for per exposure; whereas in email marketing for a few dollars, your ads reach out to thousands of people. For example, when a pizza outlet pays a few dollars ($100) to get email addresses to market, they're able to reach out to at least 10,000 customers. Just as in traditional marketing 20% turns out to be their customers. How they retain their customers and increase them depends totally on their range of products and service.

• Any startup business, small or medium size, can turn to email marketing to build customer base. Just as television commercials are watched by almost all, emails also reach a wider audience as you can send a thousand emails in one go. There are websites and software's available for this. In comparison to other methods of marketing, Email marketing is the best in terms of expense and reach.

• Also, emails can be interactive. The software can enable you to know exactly how many people have opened the email and read it and have reached your website to have a look at your products. In the interactive world, this is as good as listening to your customer. Once you know a customer has gone through your product page and has spent longer time on a particular page then you can tailor make an email and send to that specific customer. This is one of the major advantages of email marketing. You can have one to one interaction with your prospective customers.

- Data is enormously a vital element of relationship building. Once you collect data from various points you need to go through it to see if they're relevant for your business. There are several agencies that sell data for a fee. Be sure that they're genuine and get them. You can also collect data from several centers. Using CRM you can get data that can help you to target your audience.

- Once you have data, you can easily send emails and newsletters to your target audience. Once you start a conversation with your target audience, then it is within your power to convert them into customers. There is a misconception that email marketing is only for big players. That is not true. Even small businesses and home businesses can take advantage of email marketing to reach out to customers. Email marketing is a brilliant equalizer.

Attractive design

If your email is dull and boring then you can rest assured that it will be junked by the reader. Get attractive and colorful designs for your email so that its eye catchy. The design should be appropriate to your product and convey exactly what it is you're selling. This will interest the reader. With proper targeting, tracking tools, and a carefully built option list, email can be highly personalized to the needs of individual customers. Communications sent on behalf of companies from messaging solution providers can be targeted and customized using sophisticated database marketing techniques. The technology can capture and track individual responses throughout the campaign, "LEARN" more about customers from their response and purchase behavior and refine customer profiles for future communications.

See to it that your email is friendly and touches a chord with the reader. Just as how eager you are to read emails from friends and family, customize your email to sound personal. Instead of bragging about your product make your email voice what your customer wants to hear. It is here that a compelling copy is a must.

Compelling copy

There are more than ten points to note while getting copywriting done for your website. After all, you need to turn the reader into a client. Every reader is a prospective client. So your website copy should be compelling at the same time appealing to the reader.

• First and foremost, be direct and succinct. Keep sentences small and specific. Ensure that proper grammar and English is used. See to it that there is no turning of verbs into nouns. Maintaining a single voice will ensure that the reader can visualize what he is reading. Writing in a listing format makes the copy look well thought-out and lucid. The HEADLINE is responsible for most of your responses. So make sure the headline is an ATTENTION GRABBING one

• Also describe the product or services you are selling. This will make the reader curious to know more about the product and whether or not it is useful to him or her. Describe your product in details and also say how different it is from your competitors. Talk to your clients as if they're in person. Make them understand that you have thought out about all the problems that are sure to arise and have taken measures to overcome them. This will paint you as a genuine supplier and will make the reader believe you.

• Secondly, make your copywriting search engine optimized. By placing appropriate keywords throughout the pages you can optimize the site to get traffic through search engines. If you have popular keywords throughout your copy, search engines will include your website in search results for those terms. Use innovative keywords that will drive additional traffic to your site. A keyword rich content with title tag will always draw traffic to your site.

•   Once traffic is drawn, how do you convert readers into buyers? Here is where you need to be more personal and direct with your prospective client. Be honest and share all information regarding your product with your online readers. The more you tell the more you sell. Describe the benefits of your product, compare it with the competitive product and explain why it is better to buy your product. These will certainly help the reader appreciate the product and induce him to buy it.

•   In online marketing, your copyrighting is your salesman. Keep it direct; honest, and serious and most importantly, avoid humor. Your copy should be convincing and precise.

•   Add testimonials from your clients. Make them interesting in a story format. Add a picture to it. This will make it appealing as well as genuine. Storytelling has helped sell many products online. People get absorbed with stories. They visualize and get attracted to it. If you have a client who is willing to share his or her fears and apprehensions before buying your product and how your product changed his life then go for it. Add visuals as well as a video. This is sure to go well with your readers. The first line of your story should be striking and eye catching. Only then the reader will continue reading the rest of the story.

As a storyteller, your aim is to ensure that your reader feels that this product will help him or her get rid of his or her problem. Convincing your reader about this will turn him into a buyer and for that, you need an exciting and arresting story. For example:

'If I can make $1000 per day, so can you'.

This line is sure to grab the attention of the reader.

Building that relationship with your subscriber may not be easy, but it is not rocket science.

Here are a few tips that you could follow when starting your email marketing campaign:

•	Create a subject line that holds the attention of your subscriber.

•	Offer valuable new information in every email. Do not just dish out the same old jargon. Provide tips and tricks that will keep your subscriber thirsting for more.

•	Remember that this is a business letter. Personalize it but maintain a degree of formality. Remember that you are not on back-slapping terms with your subscribers.

•	Encourage feedback.

Chapter 10: The new wave - Marketing for Startups

You may think that marketing for startups is business as usual and you would be completely right but horribly wrong. Forget traditional marketing. Welcome to the rocket launch of a startup. The first thing that you must realize is that a startup has a charmed life. To be called a startup, you should grow exponentially, at an unbelievable pace. The mantra here is growth hacking. The business model also undergoes a dramatic change to the extent that it no longer resembles a business. Profitability is no longer a valid goal. In fact, startups end up with massive losses in their early years. At the same time valuations of startups hit the roof (provided you are a successful startup). Expectations are also abnormally high, almost insanely and unbelievably high. How do you market such an animal?

Now that you know the nature of a startup, you can appreciate the difficulty faced by traditional marketers to handle them. However, there are a few common elements between the run of the mill businesses and a startup.

The product, of course, still remains sacrosanct. Every startup must have a close look at the product or service which they are providing. The market for the product has to be massive – massive means covering the entire world. Products or services which succeed are generally consumed by everyone. Take the example of Uber. The idea is simple – you can call and engage a taxi anywhere and anytime. It has a product appeal since it addresses the pain points effectively. Everyone needs an Uber at some point in their life. The market for this service is massive. Uber has also spread over the world. The business model has remained the same everywhere.

What is the role of marketing in Uber? It's so obvious that you are likely to miss it. Firstly, Uber has become a brand. It is distinct from other services. You can identify an Uber taxi from a distance. You have come to believe that the service provided by Uber will be consistent anywhere in the world. You can get down at any airport and hail an Uber with your smartphone. You feel it is convenient. Uber is, in fact, a marketing effort more than anything else. It has all the elements of traditional marketing, except for the fact that it uses technology as its selling point.

The four P's of marketing are evident in Uber. The product is excellent and provides convenience far exceeding expectations. You certainly experience delight by consuming this service. Uber goes to extra length to ensure that you have a uniform experience wherever you go. What sets Uber apart from common taxis is the price point. It beats all competitors hands down. Price is probably one of the main reasons why you opt for Uber in the first place. It is affordable and dependable. Promotion of Uber has been definitely scintillating. If you look closer at Uber, you will notice that it has a great advertising and promotion campaign. Word of mouth has also played a critical role in promoting Uber. Placement of Uber has been perfect.

Keeping the above example in mind, how do you propose to market a startup? The notion of profitability should be removed from your mind when marketing a startup. The goal is to get as many customers as possible in the shortest possible time. Your marketing campaign should be able to reach out to as many people as possible. Startups by nature are bootstrapped which means they have very little cash with them. Marketing a startup is, therefore, a challenge. Digital marketing has come to the rescue of startups. Your role as a marketer is to come up with a message which looks and feels genuine. Copyrighting skills are critical in a startup environment. Organic search means keyword research, of which you should be a master. Marketers should be able to use social media like Facebook and Twitter to spread the gospel. Blogs play an important role in promoting startups. In short, you should be an expert content marketer if you wish to succeed in a startup environment.

Speaking assignments and interaction with customers are part and parcel of a startup. Startups should be good speakers or quickly learn to be one. This will be helpful when you are looking for funding, which is inevitable. Making pitches and begging for funds to accelerate the growth of your startup is quite common for startups. Marketers should be able to create powerful pitch decks for startups.

The marketing team should be ready to take on different roles in a startup. You will need different tools for launching, growth and different funding stages. Unicorns are startups who manage to mop up a billion dollars in funding. You should prepare to become a Unicorn. The whole concept of a startup is to shoot for the stars. The marketing team should believe in executing impossible tasks. It should shed the old world belief of building a business.

Startup is all about massive belief in oneself. This concept should seep into the markers. The marketing team should be able to project the image of startup in such a way that success looks imminent. It is a different matter that investors don't get carried away by PR tricks. However, you should remember that even investors are human and if they read about your startup often enough, they will start believing in the image you have created.

Growth is the byword for a startup. Marketing should focus on growth alone. Growth can only happen if you have customers. Startups realize too late that acquiring customers is quite a difficult task. 'We are giving it away free. Why shouldn't anyone become my customer?' Customers don't want anything free unless they see benefits from it. The marketing team should understand the dynamics of customer behavior to navigate their startup through turbulent waters.

Marketing for startups is a challenge as well as an opportunity to prove your worth. Running a marketing campaign for a startup gives you an adrenaline rush which is unique and worth the experience. Remember that there is no money in marketing a startup in the initial stages.

Conclusion - Putting it all together

Now that we have spent some time with marketing, it's time to sum it up.

- Marketing is essentially about providing customer delight. Savvy marketing professionals know the value of selling an experience.

- The customer is king. What motivates a customer to buy and how can marketers influence him or her is a complex task. Marketing at its meanest means focuses on the customer and nothing else. For a marketer, the customer is the bread and butter. How to know the needs of a customer? How to fulfill these needs? What are needs anyway? Marketers have to know the answers to all these questions, in order to be effective.

- Marketing is a blind profession. You don't shoot in the dark nor should you make wild claims. Market research is the bedrock of marketing.

- The internet has led to many marketing opportunities. Digital marketing, email marketing, and search marketing have become the latest power keywords in the marketing lexicon. Google has changed the way we market products and services. Amazon has transformed the marketplace. There are other digital forces changing the concept of marketing.

- The 4 P's of marketing are inviolate. Product, pricing, promotion, and placement are equally important in the scheme of things. Marketing professionals must use these judiciously to create a winning strategy.

- SWOT analysis or strength, weakness, opportunities and threats analysis is an essential and intrinsic part of marketing. A thorough analysis would result in you making fewer mistakes and lead to better marketing campaigns.

- Copywriting means a lot more than simply written words. It encompasses an understanding of the entire gamut of customer behavior and ways to attract customers.

You will become a master of marketing only if you get a feel of the actual market. Remember that you can learn swimming only by getting into the pool. Any amount of theoretical knowledge would be insufficient and inadequate. Your best tutor is practical experience. Marketing profession is full of surprises. More you learn about customers more you will be baffled by their behavior. Customers can be exasperating and difficult to understand. You will become a spectacular marketing professional if you can crack the customer's code.